MICHAEL JACKSON

ELECTRIFYING

GREG QUILL

Sidgwick & Jackson Limited
London, England

First published in Great Britain in 1988 by Sidgwick & Jackson Limited. Originally published in the United States of America in 1988 by Barron's Educational Series, Inc.

ISBN 0-283-99747-8

Typeset by Attic Typesetting Inc., Toronto, Canada

Printed by Maclean Hunter Printing, Toronto, Canada

for **Sidgwick & Jackson Limited**
1 Tavistock Chambers, Bloomsbury Way
London WC1A 2SG

PRODUCED BY GODDARD & KAMIN INC.
For Sidgwick & Jackson Limited

Book Design by: John Piazza Design

ELECTRIFYING

TABLE OF CONTENTS   **PAGE**
CHAPTER 1   The Bad Boy 8
CHAPTER 2   The Mystery Man 19
CHAPTER 3   The Motown Years 29
CHAPTER 4   The Solo Years. 39
CHAPTER 5   The Family 47
CHAPTER 6   The Rites of Passage. . . .55
CHAPTER 7   The Thriller 63
CHAPTER 8   The Victory Tour 75
CHAPTER 9   The Superstar 83

Chapter 1

The Bad Boy

Tokyo welcomes the great American legends.

Michael Jackson's BAD Tour in September 1987

Michael Jackson started the *Bad* tour in Tokyo in September 1987, amid the wildest speculation in recent show business history.

Weirdness piled on weirdness.

Entering an extremely skeptical world after three years of deep seclusion, the 29-year-old superstar let it be known that he would share his two-bedroom suite in the Japanese capital with Bubbles, his pet chimpanzee.

It was revealed soon after the August release of the *Bad* album that Jackson had acquired an agent for Bubbles, who was apparently an aspiring actor. He had also insisted on the chimp's presence at almost all the recording sessions for this extraordinary record.

Bubbles had inspired Jackson during the shooting in New York of the 14-minute *Bad* video, directed by award-winning moviemaker Martin Scorsese. The chimp entertained some 50 record industry executives and members of the media at a publicity party at Jackson's home in Encino, CA. Bubbles even slept in a crib in the super-star's room. And among the menagerie of stuffed toys that's merchandised worldwide as "Michael's Pets" the chimp's likeness is prized.

In Michael Jackson's world, there are not too many borders between the real and the imaginary. His home is a pseudo-Tudor mansion with turrets, a fully stocked candy shop, an arcade-sized electronic game room, a 30-seat screening room where cartoons run perpetually, a lobby display featuring lifelike characters from Disney's *Snow White and the Seven Dwarfs* and an enormous clock tower sparkling at night with clusters of lights. It's the "Great Amusement Park" of his dreams.

Yet all this belies the hard-nosed businessman, and brilliant musician and performer, who lives inside. Jackson, who's seen as equal parts "E.T. and Howard Hughes" by his manager, Frank Dileo, has given himself the seemingly impossible task of selling 100 million copies of *Bad*. That's more than double the sales of his previous album, *Thriller*, which is the best-selling record in pop music history.

Who's Bad

And no one really doubts that Jackson will do it—somehow. Even so, his professional abilities are far less mysterious than the man himself. Who, and what, is Michael Jackson? What makes him tick?

As for popular mythology, Jackson admits now that he's had some plastic surgery—on his nose and chin. But he claims that what changed his features most was massive weight loss, which he says was due to his strict vegetarian diet.

He also wants it known that he's had "serious" romances with actresses Tatum O'Neal and Brooke Shields. And that, as a youngster, he'd been beaten with straps by his father, Joe. He'd fight back, swinging his fists, against his father's tirades.

Those experiences, in addition to emotional scarring caused by severe teenage acne, set him up for a particularly lonely adolescence. After his first solo album, *Off the Wall*—a spectacular hit—failed to bring the real world closer to him, he'd go wandering through his neighborhood, searching for anyone who'd be his friend.

...And he's glad to be back.

Michael struts his stuff in Kansas City, 1988.

At times, he says now, he felt as if he should be at the end of his life, turning eighty.

Quincy Jones, who produced *Thriller* and co-produced *Bad*, has said that Jackson is both "the oldest man" and "the youngest kid" he knows. That's certainly borne out in the *Bad* album and the *Bad* tour. Both present a fragile child who's about to be consumed by external forces and sinister inner compulsions, but who rallies with astounding wisdom and profound humanity — and eventually survives.

Success motivates Jackson; the fear of failure paralyzes him. He's obsessed with his own standards of achievement, and even confessed once that what mattered to him most about 1979's *Off The Wall* was the four hit singles it yielded — a record that he feared Hall and Oates would break a couple of years later. They didn't.

When the album won only one Grammy, he said that his family thought he was crazy because he was weeping so much about it.

Martin Scorsese (whom Dileo selected to direct the *Bad* video over Jackson's friends George Lucas and Steven Spielberg) calls the singer "a perfectionist." Because Jackson insisted on shooting sequences again and again, the clip eventually cost $2 million. The singer didn't mind paying that price if he could infuse

Weirdness upon weirdness.

A superstar at work.

14

rock 'n' roll video with the essence of Robert Anson's novel, *Best Intentions*, on which part of the mini-movie was based.

And, of course, he was determined that the *Bad* album break new ground — in every direction. *Thriller*, as well as the backlash that followed the expensive and disastrously promoted *Victory* tour in 1984, haunted Jackson during the recording sessions. When he started in 1986, he had written more than 60 songs for the album and had already recorded dozens in his home studio. Musicians were driven crazy by the superstar as he strived to achieve absolute perfection. In fact, insiders say that many of the album's discarded song takes are identical to the finished products.

Even so, Quincy Jones was worried at the beginning of 1987 that the material lacked relevance; not passion, imagination, fire, or ideas — but some element that could convincingly deliver Jackson to the real world. *Thriller*, a fantasy that had quivered in the awful crack between adolescence and manhood, had been compelling in a way that could never be repeated now that the singer was older and, supposedly, more mature.

Michael and the band heat up the stage on BAD Tour, Tokyo.

The pelvic thrust.

Ironically, Jackson's own songs on *Bad*, songs about rock 'n' roll, sex and murder and fast cars, seem to come from television novels, movies and amusement parks — not at all from typical human experiences. Jones sought out suitable material that would somehow make Jackson more believable. He came up with Terry Britten and Graham Lyle's "Just Good Friends" — ultimately performed by Jackson and Stevie Wonder — and "Man In the Mirror," by Ballard and Siedah Garrett.

That song, with its urgent yet plaintive promise that self-improvement is the first step toward a better world, became both the centerpiece of the album and the crux of the *Bad* show. It's a powerful, revelatory song whose message resonates throughout all of Jackson's performances. And into the superstar's inner sanctum it brought singer Siedah Garrett, who performed with Jackson on *Bad's* first single, "I Just Can't Stop Loving You." (Both Barbra Streisand and Whitney Houston had declined offers to do the duet with Jackson.)

There were two final hitches in the *Bad* schedule. One was the break that Jackson took in February 1987 to shoot a stylized, gangster-era

video for "Smooth Criminal." It rolled on and on, until its budget approached $8 million, and its demands threatened to impede the June 30 delivery deadline set by Epic Records — as well as Jackson's Japanese tour, which was slated for September.

The second catastrophe — one that almost caused a deep rift between the record company and Jackson — was his choice of a cover shot. It highlighted his features in a feminine way. Epic simply refused to allow it. The final cover shot, with Jackson in buckles and leather, was snapped quickly during the *Bad* video shoot.

The *Bad* tour opened in Tokyo with all the hoopla that might have surrounded a visiting intergalactic emissary. Naturally, fans loved the shows — but critics seemed appalled by Jackson's overt sexual gestures on stage, by his reliance on violent pelvic thrusts and abundant crotch grabbing.

But when the American leg of the *Bad* tour opened in Kansas City, Mo., Feb. 23, 1988, it was tougher, leaner and far less extravagant than it had been overseas (due to extensive changes made during rehearsals in Pensacola, Fla.). Critics practically fell over themselves praising its

grace, emotional scope and "unmasked" presentation of Jackson — its unveiling of an artist who simply sang and danced better and galvanized an audience more completely than any pop performer in history.

Oh, the glitter is there, all right. The dazzling Broadway spectacle is wrapped in rock 'n' roll spangles. There's thundering technology, and massive video windows on each side of the stage — tons of raw power. There's enough non-stop action, enough energy to keep heads spinning from one montage, one image and one gesture to the next.

There's "Dirty Diana," acted out with sinister power by Jackson (the predator) and guitarist Jennifer Batten (the hunter) while an oppressive wrath — in the form of a massive, falling scaffold of light — descends from the sky.

There's the primping pop of "Heartbreak Hotel," the cheeky bravado of "Wanna Be Startin' Something," and a flashy, generous medley of The Jackson 5's Motown hits.

There's an 11-piece band that rages like a storm, yet never intrudes upon Jackson's territory, and four dancers and singers who achieve the kind of electric togetherness that most

Broadway and movie ensembles only suggest.

But what will remain when *Bad* winds down is not the memory of Jackson's obsessions (though they might have to sustain us if, as Dileo claims, this is the singer's last solo tour). Nor will it be his astonishing stamina (*Bad* goes to Europe in mid-1988, then returns to North America), his philanthropy (the Madison Square Garden show in New York on March 5 raised $500,000 for scholarships for minorities; it was one of several shows from which proceeds went to Jackson's favorite charities), nor his overwhelming need to break records—especially his own.

What's left will be the stark impression of a performer who, for most of his life, has lived and worked on the leading edge of an idea, of an artform that his work alone defines.

Michael Jackson is a fascinating character, part confection—his and ours—and part instinctive artist with a desire for perfection that's almost unknown in show business.

Look at him. He has remade himself to fit some half-baked notion of Everyman, enduring enormous pain to make himself fit everywhere, yet nowhere.

"I love you," he whispers in the darkness between concert songs in Japan, Australia, and America. But is it he who loves *us* or is it that other person, that character up there on stage? The one who suffers, who remains eternally unfulfilled? The one who has said he "bleeds" for us?

If he weren't such an astute observer of human nature, you'd say he had a complex. Maybe he does. He eats flowers in his vegetarian salads. He lives in a cocoon, surrounded by wild animals from every part of the world, hulking bodyguards and state-of-the-art TV surveillance devices.

And it's said that as a condition of his performance contract, a newly manufactured toilet (with a dated inspection seal attached) must be installed in his dressing room, under the scrutiny of a member of his entourage. There must be a new toilet for *every* show on the *Bad* tour, and it can only be used by Jackson.

Yes, it's easy to make fun of Michael Jackson. That's partly his fault; he's so frighteningly withdrawn that at times he seems incapable of speech. And any man who can offer the world solutions to destructive human traits—as self-assuredly as he does in "Bad" and "Beat It"—would surely be good for more than the odd mumbled homily, no?

Only if life reflected art.

Michael Jackson, more than any other entertainer, is living art—a creation of his own childhood sensibilities. He only really comes alive on stage, under the lights, amid the razzle-dazzle of mind-boggling technology. And there he simply exhausts himself. Left off stage for too long, his mind tears away from reality, like a shadow fleeing the sun.

What's amazing about Michael Jackson is not his sexual duplicity, his enormous wealth, his sculpted face, the 40 million copies of *Thriller* sold between 1982 and now or the 12 million copies of *Bad* sold during the first few months of its release. It's his almost inhuman dedication to the art of performance, to dance and music, mime and acting, to the very powers of illusion.

And what's all this dedication about? Why the sacrifices, the pain, the bleeding?

It's there, in the spotlight, that image of a half-naked animal/man running against time, against history, against our basic instincts—running toward what he believes is a better world.

Chapter 2

The
Mystery Man

There's no way we can get to the nub of Michael Jackson. He's a chameleon, a freak of his and our creation, no surer of his own destiny than we are of his true nature.

Yet some things are known. He performs as if his life depended on it, at a level beyond fun and profit, beyond the mere need for adoration, beyond standards approached by conventional stars. Performance isn't work for Michael Jackson, but a self-fulfilling act, the necessary proof of his existence, a benediction.

But let's not get carried away. He is, after all, flesh and blood. He may remain one of the greatest human mysteries of all time, an eccentric comparable to Howard Hughes or William Randolph Hearst. But he is tangible, and, under the tabloid glaze, he's a man with a story. The trouble is, he may be too big a story, his dimensions may simply be beyond our understanding.

Still, let's start with what we know.

By the end of 1984, Jackson's third solo album, *Thriller*, had sold an unprecedented 38.5 million copies worldwide, at a rate of 300,000 a week for almost two years. It remains, and will likely

BAAAD as ever.

Michael waits for a scene to be set up for the BAD video.

Michael in 1988: tougher, leaner…

Eddie Van Halen joins the Jacksons on stage during their Victory Tour.

remain until another Michael Jackson record surpasses it, the best-selling album in history.

In statistical terms, he outranks all other music stars from the past generation, even those who set the standards to which he has aspired. As a matter of fact, when he was only 14, Michael Jackson was a millionaire.

Without exception, no showbusiness family has been as successful or as enduringly popular as the Jackson brothers, the last great group fostered by Detroit-based Motown Records during the ascendancy of popular black music in America in the late 1960s.

It was The Jackson 5 who realized the epic dream of Motown founder Berry Gordy, Jr. — his vision of delivering palatable black pop to the white American masses. It was a dream not unlike the one that sparked the creation of rock 'n' roll itself, in the person of Elvis Presley, just months before Michael Jackson was born on Aug. 29, 1958. The possibility of a fusion of propulsive black rhythms and white, working-class sensibilities had long enthralled Elvis' Memphis producer Sam Phillips. And Gordy's creation, a generation later, was to prove no less revolutionary.

The Jackson 5's beginnings, however, were inauspicious, despite four consecutive Number One singles, starting with "I Want You Back" in 1969.

Essentially a novelty act brought to Motown not by Diana Ross, as legend has it, but by record company partner Gladys Knight, the quintet from Gary, Ind. was at first perceived as another manufactured product in Gordy's "assembly line." The group was fronted by a prepubescent dynamo — the ever exuberant Michael Jackson — who spun and jumped, dipped and pirouetted, moved like a tiny James Brown and sang his little heart out. At first The Jackson 5 was pure teenybopper fare, even though its early records displayed more than the prerequisite amount of musical intelligence and harmonic wit. This talent, unlike much of Gordy's professionally backed roster and unlike any of the group's "imitators," was for real.

Largely because of Michael Jackson, The Jackson 5 soon imprinted itself on the American consciousness. It matured quickly, and passed from young hands to the great masses, transcending all race and age barriers in its appeal. In the early 1970s, a popular kids' cartoon series was even based on The Jackson 5's imaginary exploits.

Within three years, the Jacksons had moved into more sophisticated forms of pop and soul, and by the middle of the decade, into high-tech disco, to which they added both glamour and personality.

A scene from the BAD video—directed by Martin Scorsese.

On the set of the BAD video which eventually cost 2 million dollars.

Michael who's seen as equal parts "ET and Howard Hughes" by his manager.

Buckles and band-aids.

By the time Michael Jackson was 14, the group had sold 10 million albums. At 17, he was leader of the most popular black pop group in history. That success came at a price, of course. No child can foresee the effects of such extraordinary wealth and fame, nor sense what he has missed along the way. If Jackson grew up physically before America's very eyes, his emotional and spiritual development remained constricted by the only realities he knew — his family, the recording studio and the touring regimen. Years later, he'd try to recreate and perpetuate a fantasy childhood he never really had. Still, back in 1969, no one could have guessed that The Jackson 5 was more than a money-making gimmick.

Michael Joseph Jackson, the seventh of nine children, was born and partly raised in Gary, Ind. Hunkered down between Lake Michigan and the Calumet River, Gary is a bourgeois industrial town whose major product in the postwar era was steel. During that period, it was also a city growing in self-importance and new wealth — bulging with both poor black laborers from the South, now in agricultural decline, and with slick "money men" from the North and the East. Gary was also well connected, via the river,

the Great Lakes and new freeways, to America's burgeoning cultural revolution — including music. Bleak in appearance, this was nonetheless fertile territory.

Jackson's father, Joseph, married his mother, Katherine, when she was 16. He took her from her native Chicago back to Gary, where he worked as a crane operator in a steel plant.

Children came quickly: Maureen in 1950; Sigmond Esco (nicknamed Jackie) in 1951; Toriano Adarryl (Tito) in 1953; Jermaine La Jaune in 1954; second daughter LaToya in 1955; Marlon David in 1957; and Michael in 1958. His arrival seems to have interrupted the process; Steven Randall (Randy) wasn't born until 1965, followed by Janet in 1967.

Right from the cradle, the Jackson children were united by music. Katherine taught them folk songs and spirituals. Joe played guitar in a rhythm 'n' blues band called The Falcons, whose members included his brothers. He brought home the blues and rock 'n' roll of Chuck Berry, Muddy Waters, and B.B. King, among others.

There was always music of some kind in the Jackson house. The children sang together spontaneously, usually with Maureen at the piano and

first Joe, then Tito, on guitar. Years later, the family was to credit the failure of its TV set with the need to entertain themselves by singing the standards and the hits of the day — "Under The Boardwalk," "Cotton Fields," "Twist and Shout," "You Are My Sunshine." The boys listened to The Falcons perform and rehearse, and they soon learned to accompany their own harmonies with the band's discarded instruments — a tambourine, an old saxophone, bongos — which took the place of toys the family could not afford.

It wasn't long before Joe realized his children, particularly Jermaine, who'd begun playing bass, and Tito, were unusually gifted. He quit The Falcons and started teaching the boys the rudiments of music, elaborate harmonies and stage presentation — mostly tricks culled from local bar and concert acts.

Encouraged by his sons' expertise and enthusiasm, Joe Jackson gave up his job in the mid-1960s and tackled the serious work of grooming them to be professionals. He bought them second-hand instruments and amplifiers, much to Katherine's chagrin, and taught them all he knew, including choreographed dance steps.

Michael Jackson, a natural mimic, wasn't part of the group when it first started performing its versions of current r 'n' b hits in Gary. But during rehearsals one afternoon, he astonished his father and brothers with a hilarious imitation of soul godfather James Brown. He capped it off with a cheeky takeoff of his brother's (Jermaine's) vocal tics. His appeal was powerful, and he was recruited for duty, first as a cute novelty on bongos, and then as lead singer and dancer.

"He was so energetic that at five years old he was like a leader," Jackie Jackson once told *Rolling Stone* magazine. "The audience ate it up. The speed was the thing. He would see somebody do something and he could do it right away."

"It was sort of frightening. He was so young. He didn't go out and play much. I don't know where he got it. He just *knew*."

Michael Jackson, however, paints a different picture. In a rare interview in the 1970s, he said, "We used to rehearse all the time in Gary; every day when we came home from school. My father used to make us keep going, and he put it in our heads that practice makes perfect. I used to come home from school at three and everything would be set up in the living room, the drums and all, and we practised until night. And we kept on and kept on. We used to wonder, 'Will we have a show?'"

At seven years old, Michael Jackson was a dazzling dancer, probably the product of his father's fantasies. He had already taken control of the group's choreography from brother Jackie. And by 1965, The Jackson 5 — Tito, Marlon, Jermaine, Jackie and Michael, augmented for a short time by cousins Johnnie Jackson on drums and Ronnie Rancifer on piano — were a local phenomenon. They won talent contests and made considerable money at pass-the-hat shows.

It became obvious to Joe Jackson that he had a rare gem in Michael Jackson, a potent and naturally charismatic performer who simply thrived on applause and was hell-bent on perfection. And Joe — now chauffeur, manager, roadie and chaperone for his sons — exploited it for all it was worth. In a borrowed Volkswagen van, he took the group to showcases and guest spots in clubs in New York, including the famed Apollo Theater, and to The Uptown in Philadelphia.

Fittingly, it was at The Apollo, mecca to urban black musicians, where Gladys Knight first spotted The Jackson 5. She later sang their praises to Motown's Berry Gordy, Jr.

Diana Ross, who performed with the group at a 1968 "Soul Weekend" concert series in Gary, reinforced Knight's opinion.

"I saw so much of myself as a child in Michael," she recalled years later. "He was performing *all* the time. That's the way I was. He could be my son."

Michael Jackson wasn't always quite as innocuous and cute. By 1967, he'd learned to scoop up five- and ten-dollar bills during his dazzling on-stage dips, performing ever more amazing feats for larger bills. Earlier, when he was only six, he'd occasionally get tangled in the skirts of a stripper who was sharing a bill with the group. He cheekily invented his own peek-a-boo parody on the spot.

There was more to this boy than met the eye, as Berry Gordy would soon discover.

Chapter 3 **The Motown Years**

Gordy, under whose guidance the Motown Corporation had become the largest and most
successful black-owned company in the world,
signed the Jacksons after a pool-side audition at
his home. He suggested the family move to
California, where for the next year he would
support them during the extensive grooming
process he believed they needed.

Capping off a spectacular
year—Jackson receives 8
Grammys.

Michael Jackson would later recall, "I was a veteran before I was a teenager." He was 10 when Motown took him on. Still, the young boy was given much compensation for his hard work. The family's new home in Encino was a palace of delights, a 12-room stucco bungalow set in a secluded compound guarded by dogs and an elaborate alarm system. It had a swimming pool, small basketball court, badminton court, guest house and pool room, plus an archery range and servants' quarters.

Gordy's efforts were quickly rewarded. After the regional hit, "I'm A Big Boy Now," which the group had recorded for the small and under-funded Chicago Steeltown label, The Jackson 5's first Motown single was released in November 1969. Called "I Want You Back," it immediately began climbing the charts.

Like no record before it, "I Want You Back" crossed race, age and class barriers, winning an enormous audience that included flower children and students, black and white preteens, urban soul aficionados and middle-American families. The song, with Michael Jackson's urgent, pleading soprano right up front, was the center piece of the group's first album — *Diana Ross Presents The Jackson Five*, released the

Michael with friends Lionel and Brenda Richie and close pal Liz Taylor.

Michael, in happier
times, with Paul and
Linda McCartney and
Gary Coleman.

Michael in a pensive
mood in a new soft
drink commercial.

following year. The album spawned four chart-topping singles: "ABC", which won a Grammy in 1970 for best song of the year and knocked The Beatles' "Let It Be" off the top of the charts in April, "The Love You Save" and "I'll Be There," which were Number One records — selling more than one million copies each in the United States alone; and "The Love You Save," which surpassed "The Long And Winding Road" in June.

By the summer of 1970, Michael Jackson's childhood was over before it had really begun. Processed by the Motown machine, he would no longer dance or move like James Brown. A new kind of choreography, professionally charted and based on the family's natural gestures and sense of timing, was developed for the stage. It was put to stunning use when The Jackson 5 made its national TV debut on *The Ed Sullivan Show* to coincide with the launch of "I Want You Back."

More importantly, Michael and Jermaine Jackson, as leaders, were put through a grueling series of tutorials designed to take all the personality out of their responses to the media. Individual opinions were forbidden; bland answers, or better still, complete avoidance of any subject that could be construed as controversial, were encouraged. Michael Jackson's innate charm and wit, his natural curiosity, his cheekiness and sharp intelligence were slowly stripped away, at least from his public persona.

A star and almost a millionaire at 11, Michael Jackson was becoming someone else — a

Michael accompanies Sophia Loren.

Beating it in Kansas City.

younger version of the often painfully reticent, reclusive and evasive man he is today.

First his father, then Gordy's Motown machine, constructed a new personality for him, one with impenetrable armor, one whose real passions would remain locked away forever.

The process extended to The Jackson 5's creative life as well. Though it was a self-contained musical unit, the group simply sang over what had been prewritten and recorded for it by Motown's "Corporation" — a close-knit circle of writers, musicians, arrangers and producers in charge of changing Motown's musical image from light and frivolous to funky and relevant.

The Jacksons, mere newcomers, had no say in what was done on their behalf and they made no contribution aside from their distinctive vocals on an all but finished product. Lost in the excitement sparked by those first singles was the awful irony that this tiny, perfect singer had learned his craft so well that his performance conveyed all the intensity of adult emotions even though he had no idea what such "grown-up" lyrics meant.

Things were moving almost too quickly. Within nine months, the previously unknown black group reached the Number One spot on the American charts and stayed there for an unprecedented 10 weeks. Obviously, Gordy's intuition

had paid off; the Jackson's success proved there was a giant hole in the American music market. The group moved to fill it, taking an exceedingly theatrical, Motown-produced roadshow across America and to Europe.

Wherever The Jackson 5 played, there was teenage pandemonium unseen since The Beatles. Magazines dedicated whole issues to the act, and the group even published its own quarterly fanzine. TV projected them to untold millions in 1971 and 72 — first via their own ABC special, *Goin' Back To Indiana*, then in an animated cartoon series, *The Jackson Five*, which used their likenesses and their music but not their speaking voices. The recording schedule was hectic — three albums, *I Want You Back*, *ABC* and *Third Album* all cracked the Top 5.

In 1971, the Jackson brothers were honored by their hometown and Gary mayor Richard Hatcher, whose candidacy they had endorsed, with two benefit shows. Jan. 31 was proclaimed Jackson Day; a street in the city was renamed Jackson 5 Street; the house in which they had grown up was proclaimed a historic building; they were given the keys to the city; and they received a special prize from the University of Indiana for giving "hope to the young."

In September of '71, the family was honored in

the Congressional Record for capturing the nation's imagination and upholding American family ideals.

Much has been made of the strength of the Jackson family. Indeed, they became symbols of the emerging black middle class in the United States; they were educated, industrious, wholesome, religious capitalists who remained apparently unspoiled by their sudden success. Even as millions clamored for them, they were bound by normal obligations: Sharing household chores, cleaning, washing dishes and, above all, completing their homework, more to please Joe and Katherine than a succession of highly paid private tutors.

Bassist and second singer Jermaine quickly emerged as the group's first real sex symbol, overshadowing Jackie and Tito. Michael and Marlon, cute as they were, were too young to be heartthrobs.

Still, Michael Jackson had his share of adoration. His angelic face, passionate soprano, magic footwork, speed and nerve captured most of the kudos the group won in those first two years. It wasn't long before Gordy realized he had not one act on his hands, but two.

In 1971, when Michael Jackson was 13, Motown released his first solo album, *Got To Be There*, which won him a Grammy for vocalist of the year. *Ben, Music And Me, Forever, Michael* and *The Best Of Michael Jackson* followed in rapid succession until 1975, when most of the Jacksons parted company with Motown. Only Jermaine stayed; he married Gordy's daughter, Hazel.

By then, both Michael Jackson and the group had outgrown their teenybopper beginnings without betraying their vast audience. The Jacksons were turning to disco and its tough-edged offshoot, funk, which gave them new impetus. They also found a mature audience as large and potent as the one that had swept them to the top of the charts initially.

Chapter 4 **The Solo Years**

But something else had been going on with Michael Jackson. "Got To Be There," the title track of his first solo album, offered the first real glimpse of the man he would become. A sensitive, wistful ballad sung in an aching voice, it shared much with the earlier "I'll Be There". There was a deep, isolated passion here, an anguish reflected also in "She's Out Of My Life," from *Off The Wall*, his later solo album. That song, no longer a mere weeper but a declaration of overpowering despair, is still in his stage repertoire and remains one of his all-time favorites.

It's clear from these very early solo records that Michael Jackson's psyche was developing in a different way from that of his brothers and sisters. At 13, his only experience of the real world was through an industrial filter, from behind walls, from windows and television, from physical distances that enforced a deep sense of alienation.

While he was the idol of millions, his emotional progress was slow. He was being driven inward by the pressures of work, by the intense scrutiny of the media that devoured and dissected him daily — and served up a distorted pasted-together picture. As a young, impressionable boy, Jackson must have been quite puzzled by this at once familiar, yet frighteningly untrue image.

The Encino regimen did little to help him relate to realities outside the family compound and the music business. Normal as his parents tried to keep their home life, the boys' schedule meant that when they were off the road they had

Critics talk of "awesome interpretations."

Michael ready to shoot a commercial.

to attend a nearby private school with two or three dozen other children of the local elite. On tour they were accompanied by a state-appointed tutor required for minors under the California Child Labor Act. In every aspect of their lives they were isolated, removed from or exalted beyond the reach of their peers.

No one could have survived all this completely unscathed. But because of his age, Michael Jackson felt the pressure most acutely. For family and business reasons, and because he knew of no alternatives, his course was set. He withdrew

into a fantasy world, to his room adorned with
tiny cutouts of cartoon characters and space-
men, and to his pet menagerie.

There's a quality of deepening despair on
those first records, though it was washed away
with bubbly novelties like "Rockin' Robin," "I
Wanna Be Where You Are" and a masterful
cover version of Bill Withers' "Ain't No Sunshine."

Then, in mid-1972, he recorded the theme
song for the psycho-thriller *Ben*, a disturbing
movie about a love-starved boy's relationship

Every performance is a
thriller.

43

with a rat capable of profound understanding and gruesome murder.

The song was a slice of pure white sentimentality. There was nothing in either its construction or lyrics that might have attracted Jackson or had anything in common with his previous work. He recorded "Ben," so it's said, for sound business reasons; a smash movie would almost certainly give the young singer a huge hit and boost him further into the mainstream.

His every phrase filled with profound caring.

The truth machine.

A love song to a psychopathic rat is not the kind of composition that most serious singers would care to have lingering on for the rest of their lives. Few performers could even sing it with a straight face.

But Jackson did. He sang it straight from the heart, his unwavering soprano full and pure, his every phrase tinged with a profound caring. It was a chilling performance, one that clearly had a focus for him and probably made the movie more popular than it deserved to be.

What's especially remarkable is that since the song was promoting a movie that many people found tasteless, it was banned on most American radio stations when first released. Yet, by the end of 1972, "Ben" became the Number One record in the United States — Michael's first chart-topper as a solo performer.

One revealing aside to the "Ben" story appeared in *Crawdaddy* magazine in 1977. Jackson loved rats. In fact, he said, he used to raise them in a cage when he first moved to California. But one misty night he noticed that the adults, as most caged rodents will do, were eating their young.

"I got sick of looking at it all," he said, laughing. "I left their cage outside. The rats still alive froze to death..."

Chapter 5 **The Family**

Michael with his pet llama which was part of an extensive private zoo installed at the family's Encino home in 1982.

The Jackson 5 recorded four more albums for Motown before falling apart in late 1975: *Get It Together*, *Dancing Machine*, *Moving Violation* and *The Jackson Five Anthology*. In June of that year, Michael Jackson's solo single, "Just A Little Bit Of You," and The Jackson 5's "Forever Came Today" were both in the American Top 20.

Asked once if the group resented his assumption of leadership, Michael Jackson answered, "Each person has a thing that he does. I sing and dance and the other brothers sing and dance, but I sing lead. I've been doing this since I was five years old onstage and I feel it's something God gave me to do. I'm the one who sings lead. I'm thankful to be chosen. They kind of understand it, and accept it because that's what I do."

Not coincidentally, his self-assurance echoes advice given to him by Ed Sullivan backstage, when the group made its first national TV appearance: "Never forget that God gave you this talent." Michael Jackson has never since doubted that for him performance is a mission.

Outwardly the Jacksons seemed to be typical California boys, though members of a very select community that included Berry Gordy III and Diana Ross' brother, Chico. Tito, who preferred flashy clothes and big hats, was the only one you could call boisterous. But even his inclinations were reserved for football games, pool parties and other social events with the "Motown crowd," a group of about 30 performers and businessmen close to and including Gordy, Ross and Marvin Gaye.

They knew they led a charmed life, and most of the boys, particularly Michael, were curious about the real problems of urban black Americans. Harlem fascinated Michael Jackson in a way that Gary, with all its steely toughness, never did. He'd question anyone who'd lived there for details and reacted with wonder, as if to fairy tales.

It's been said that the yearning in his best work, the yearning the world first heard in

"My father used to make us keep going and he put it in our heads that practice makes perfect. We used to wonder, 'Will we have a show?'"

"Ben," is for a black America he never really knew or understood. He had spent his life in a kind of limbo, somewhere between cracks. It's easy to see that later he saw no obstacle to re-making himself in the image that had begun imprinting itself on his consciousness.

That image probably became ingrained during his first close encounter with the business of movies. In 1972, Gordy began producing *Lady Sings The Blues*, the life story of 1930s jazz and blues diva Billie Holiday, in which he'd cast Michael Jackson's willing mentor, Diana Ross. Regardless of the final product, it was the perfection of movie-making, itself, that dazzled Jackson. There was nothing short-lived here. Unlike even television, nothing was committed to film or delivered to the public until it was perfect, or

as close to perfect as the artists in front of and behind the cameras could make it. This was fail-safe performance art that could last forever; images of life ever unfolding anew, way into the future. Its possibilities would later consume him.

In the meantime, his world was expanding. While on tour in Europe, he explored classical art and literature, museums and architecture that he thought only existed in school books. A sense of his own fragility overcame the young singer in 1972 and '73, especially after he performed in Osaka, Japan, Hiroshima and Tokyo's Imperial Palace. On the same tour he visited India, where he discovered the power and gentle grace of the Hindu religion.

The group also played in Australia that year, and Jackson said that his most lingering memory was not the thousands of modern-day, white fans who attended The Jackson 5 concerts; but, rather, a barbecue hosted by leaders of the country's ancient aborigine people.

BAD Tour—Tokyo, 1987. Michael emerges after 3 years of seclusion.

Of all their overseas journeys, it was a 10-day trip to Senegal, West Africa, in 1973 that remained with him and his brothers the longest. On his return, he said, "I don't want the blacks ever to forget that this is where we came from and where our music comes from. I want us to remember."

Five years later, the horror of the slave cells they saw on Gore Island, off Senegal, returned to the boys when they were invited to perform in South Africa for untold amounts of money. It wasn't difficult to turn down the offer.

Back home, popular music entered a new phase in 1974. Disco, an expertly manufactured, high-tech, lowbrow form of dance music, was filling the club scene. The Jackson 5's "Dance Machine" single predated the worst and even managed to elevate expectations for disco. But the album of the same name was far from a critical success. Still trying to bridge the gap between their teenybopper period and the new

He's *BAAAD* . . . .

There was always music of some kind in the Jackson house. The children sang together spontaneously.

music they believed they had in them, the brothers began to pressure Gordy to let them take responsibility for their own work. They wanted to write, to commit to tape the material they'd been recording in their Encino home studio since 1972.

Gordy, increasingly busy with projects outside the Motown record division, was in no mood to listen. He wouldn't relinquish artistic control, but he did relax the reins enough to let Joe Jack-

son resume management of the band's performances. The Jackson 5's triumphant first engagement at the new MGM Grand Hotel in Las Vegas was Joe's first power move in years.

Rumors of The Jackson 5's decision to leave Gordy and Motown in late 1975 spelled the end for the powerful label, which had had a virtual monopoly on black music in America for a decade. Gladys Knight and The Pips had already gone, and so had The Four Tops, The Temptations and The Isley Brothers. The Supremes and Martha Reeves had faded from view and the roster was meager.

The Jacksons signed with the Epic label, a division of CBS Records, and a long, unpleasant lawsuit followed. "Creative differences" were cited as the cause of the rift. But, in fact, the "differences" were both financial and artistic. Motown's method of operation was to have its artists record many more tracks than were needed for a record album, shelve what didn't make it on to vinyl and deduct the recording costs from royalties. It was a legitimate practice, but the Jacksons felt they should have more in the bank—considering their sales and their pre-eminence. However, Gordy was eventually awarded $600,000 for damages as well as rights to The Jackson 5 name. Nevertheless, the industry sympathized with the group's wish to record its own material and with its claim that innate talent, not Gordy's extensive grooming, fueled its success.

Jermaine Jackson, torn between his family and his devotion to Hazel Gordy, opted to stay on and launched a successful solo career. Michael Jackson, who had occupied the spot on stage that was nearest to Jermaine, admitted to missing him for "a long time."

Hopes were high. The group had a new name, The Jacksons; a new member, Randy; and a new vision. But it didn't yet have its freedom. The first two Epic albums — *The Jacksons* in 1976 and *Goin' Places* in 1977 — were written and primarily produced by Kenny Gamble and Leon Huff, the engineers of the lush, polished "Philadelphia Sound" that gained prominence in the mid-1970s. The first album sold 500,000 copies, but the second was a commercial failure.

There were several Jackson contributions to those records, and, in retrospect, they were the most outstanding cuts. Again, the brothers bit the bullet and kept their best for later. They

Michael in a rare moment of relaxation.

survived this period largely on TV appearances, including regular spots on *American Bandstand*, *The Midnight Special* and *Soul Train*. And with sisters Maureen and LaToya, they landed *The Jacksons* TV series on CBS in the summer of 1976 and winter of the following year.

If the face of American music was suddenly confused, so was life in the Jackson home. Tito, Jackie and Marlon had already married and all had children. Randy, now a sex symbol, had left home. And Michael was left in Encino with his parents, Janet, who was now on the TV show *Facts Of Life*, and LaToya.

During the next two years, Michael Jackson preferred the friendship of movie stars over that of his musical peers. He also was the victim of often malicious gossip concerning his sexual orientation — based no doubt on his extreme shyness and on social evidence that he was not the proud young stud his brothers had become. The rumors first shocked, then amused him, especially since he'd been seen around Los Angeles with Tatum O'Neal, the adolescent daughter of actor Ryan O'Neal.

He declared more than once that he wasn't gay, and that homosexuals didn't bother him. Nevertheless, the taunts continued, and they still persist today.

In 1978, when he was 19, came independence and vindication. For a year, the brothers, — particularly Michael and Randy, — had been "coached" in Encino by keyboardist/arranger Greg Phillinganes, a former member of Stevie Wonder's session ensemble. He helped them put together songs and a style that marked a turning point. With the release that year of the *Destiny* album, The Jacksons displayed an astonishing originality and new-found energy in both production and composition of their music.

On a roll with that change, Joe Jackson took management reins from former colleague Richard Arons and handed them to the hard-nosed, well-versed team of Ron Weisner and Freddy DeMann.

Destiny sold more than two million copies in the United States and yielded two disco-style singles, "Blame It On The Boogie" (a non-original), "Shake Your Body" (by Michael and Randy) and Michael's autobiographical ballad, "Bless His Soul," a plea for understanding from a boy who confesses that he's "used" and "confused" and offers himself "at beck and call."

That song could hardly have summed up Michael Jackson's feelings at the time. In late 1977, he landed the role of Scarecrow in the Motown/Universal motion picture, *The Wiz*. This all-black, rock 'n' roll version of the classic *Wizard Of Oz*, would star Diana Ross — playing the role originated by Judy Garland, whom Jackson called his soul mate. He was ecstatic.

The Wiz had already been a Broadway hit, with teenage star Stephanie Mills in the Garland role. It won seven Tony awards during its year-long run. The show appealed in every way to Jackson's sense of fantasy — and his belief in spiritual redemption and the fulfillment of a prophesied return to basic morality, a tenet of the Church of the Seventh Day Adventists (Jehovah's Witnesses).

He moved to New York (with LaToya as a chaperone) to shoot the movie and literally threw himself into the part. There were cold, New York winter days when some dancers actually had to leave the set, but Michael had to be pried from his costume long after shooting had stopped.

At night, in his Manhattan apartment, Jackson watched Spencer Tracy and Katharine Hepburn movies, the dance routines of Fred Astaire and the classic silent comedies of Charlie Chaplin for inspiration.

An inexperienced actor, he looked to Astaire and Chaplin as role models and soul mates. His own dancing, it has been observed, most resembles Astaire's in its complete originality and gracefulness, and in its suggestion of an almost sexless, but nonetheless potent character.

And Chaplin, whom Jackson would often imitate on the set, had revealed on film a profound understanding of human nature. It was gained from his own painful childhood, when he'd been overshadowed, and then abandoned by an alcoholic father and a psychotic mother.

Jackson's life had been quite different. Yet he adored Chaplin for his ability to recreate his confusion and melancholy on screen. In fact, Chaplin would become a kind of ghostly counterpart for every "character" Jackson played, from Scarecrow up to and including the boy in the "Bad" video.

Chapter 6

The Rites
of Passage

The Wiz was a $60-million flop, the most expensive musical movie disaster in history. One hit emerged: "Ease On Down The Road," a duet featuring Michael Jackson and Diana Ross, who, at 34, was simply unconvincing as the black Dorothy. She was generally blamed for the movie's failure.

But the experience wasn't a waste for Jackson, who liked The Wiz and considered it superior to the original. Acting enthralled him, not so much the creation of a character, but the actual assumption of it. He wasn't an actor, he said at the time, but "a believer." By way of film, he was able to slip at will into his fantasies, where he could survive forever in celluloid perfection.

He also came out of his shell in New York during the shoot. In addition to Diana Ross and Tatum O'Neal, he hobnobbed with such stars as Mick Jagger, Stephanie Mills, Andy Warhol, Liza Minnelli, to whom he warmed immediately and whose mother, Judy Garland, he had adored from afar. Mills maintained, for some time, that Jackson and she had been in love.

The association that would have the most powerful effect on him in future years was also made during his time with The Wiz. Composer/arranger/producer Quincy Jones, the movie's musical director and a 30-year studio and session veteran, told outsiders that he believed Jackson's performance was "mind-boggling" — and he took the young singer under his wing.

Jones had impeccable credentials. In the 1950s and '60s, he had produced jazz greats Art Farmer and Clifford Brown; had arranged soul/gospel pioneer Ray Charles' classics "I Can't Stop Loving You" and "Let The Good Times Roll;" and had even produced a pop hit, "It's My Party," for Lesley Gore. Moreover, he set a standard in writing and producing stunning movie soundtracks for such groundbreakers as Sidney Lumet's The Pawnbroker, Norman Jewison's In The Heat Of The Night and Richard Brooks' In Cold Blood. In the business of both music and movies, he was a giant.

And he believed in Michael Jackson passion-

The way she makes him feel!

Michael with Jane Fonda and award for the album "Off the Wall" in 1980

ately, saying he was "a truth machine" who had achieved a rare balance between "the wisdom of a 60-year-old and the enthusiasm of a child." With the release of the *Destiny* album and a world tour looming, Jackson was in no position to resume his solo career for some time yet. But when the time came, he asked Jones to recommend a producer.

Without hesitation, Jones suggested himself.

When *Off The Wall*, his first Epic solo album, was released in late 1979, the world saw and heard a new Michael Jackson. Physically, he had grown, and his voice seemed to have both deepened and extended in range. (Jones deliberately lowered the keys of most of the songs that Jackson brought to him to achieve this end.) His nose, once broad, was noticeably thinner and upturned. His Afro had been close-cropped, and his demeanor was composed and almost deliberately choreographed, like a model's, even in casual encounters.

During this time, he also became increasingly reclusive, and was particularly reticent about

"The wisdom of a 60-year-old and the enthusiasm of a child."

He'll rock with you.

giving interviews to the print media, which he believed manipulated his words in ways that television and radio couldn't.

Between albums, as his brothers withdrew to their families, hobbies, friends and nonmusical pursuits, Jackson immersed himself in music. He studied it and dedicated himself to it with almost monastic devotion. Curiously, his musical heroes had little in common with his vision of pop, which now embraced video and movies, punk, funk and hard rock. Not so curiously, they were all leaders in their fields, originators of performance styles and they enjoyed enduring fame: Frank Sinatra, Mel Torme, Tony Bennett, Nat "King" Cole, Paul McCartney, Stevie Wonder, Earth Wind & Fire, The Isley Brothers, among others.

When he started recording *Off The Wall*, in November, 1978, Michael Jackson had only one real aim. This record must not, he instructed Jones, sound like The Jacksons.

Off The Wall exceeded all expectations. It eventually sold more than eight million copies and broke music industry records by yielding four Top 10 singles: the Grammy-winning "Don't Stop 'Til You Get Enough," "Rock With You" (both hit Number One), the title track and "She's Out Of My Life," which moved Michael so much during the sessions that Jones was forced to postpone the final recording at least three times.

It was during this period that Jackson and Paul McCartney cemented a profitable friendship that endured until Jackson seized control of the

Beatles' song publishing catalog in 1986. At a party hosted by McCartney and his wife, Linda, aboard the Queen Mary in Los Angeles in 1977, the powerful composer casually offered Jackson a song, actually only a fragment. But Jackson lost McCartney's phone number. The song, "Girlfriend," surfaced soon after on McCartney's *London Town* LP. Jackson recalled it, and tracked McCartney down for permission to use the song on his own album. "Girlfriend" was also released as a single in Britain.

McCartney took a strong liking to Jackson and during the next couple of years shared his many business insights, chiefly those dealing with song publishing. The Beatles, because of a number of poor decisions made on their behalf in the 1960s, had lost control of their song catalog — by far the most valuable in pop music history. McCartney, George Harrison and the estate of John Lennon still received writers' royalties for the songs they'd composed, but the payments equaled only half of what the songs actually earned. The publishing royalties were now going to eccentric Australian businessman Robert Holmes a Court, who had secured the catalog in the 1970s from British entertainment mogul Sir Lew Grade.

Though McCartney was one of the wealthiest men in the business, still an active writer and an acquisitive publisher — having bought the rights to the valuable songs of his hero, the late Buddy Holly — he could not raise enough cash to buy back The Beatles' material. He was working on it, he assured Jackson. And some day he'd do it.

Jackson devoured all this inside information, imparted willingly by one of his own heroes and now a close friend. Without ever telling McCartney, he began studying everything he could about the music publishing business. Jackson had plans of his own.

Meanwhile, there were more pressing concerns. *Off The Wall* had rocketed Jackson to new heights. He was making new and important friends. He shared a cabin with actress Jane Fonda (who had used one of Jackson's earlier songs on her record-breaking *Work Out* home exercise video), and her father, Henry, during the shooting of *On Golden Pond*.

"He's like one of the walking wounded," she said later. "An extremely fragile person."

Later he would also befriend Katharine Hepburn, who also became a mentor and coach.

And Epic was anxious for another Jacksons' album to complete a record-breaking two in a row.

Triumph, aptly named, fulfilled the company's dreams. Produced by the brothers themselves and written largely by Michael, Jackie and Randy, it sold more than two million copies by mid-1981 — spawning the Top 10 singles: "Lovely One," Michael's "Heartbreak Hotel" and "Can You Feel It," a joyful tribute to brotherly love that was accompanied by the group's first full-length video.

In the summer of 1981, The Jacksons kicked off a 36-city North American tour featuring a show (designed by Michael) of unprecedented proportions. For the first time, video was incorporated into the performance, together with a spectacular magic act — in which the boys appeared as Greek deities sprinkling gold on the masses. Reinforcing the notion that Michael Jackson and his brothers possessed a magic power that could change the world, such illusions would recur years later in both the *Victory* and the *Bad* shows.

The *Triumph* tour grossed more than $5 million, the most the group had ever received in ticket receipts, and it yielded *The Jacksons Live!* LP, which was released the following year.

Despite the tour's success, the live album was deemed a failure; and on its heels came rumors of a final split between Michael Jackson and his brothers.

Chapter 7   **The Thriller**

Immortal ...

...or all too mortal.

The following two years were mainly spent preparing the *Thriller* album with Quincy Jones. Jackson kept a low profile, though the public was becoming increasingly hungry for some intimacy with him.

Passing from adolescence to manhood was difficult for Jackson. He resented all intrusions, hated any real contact with the world and referred to his rare encounters with fans as "spaghetti passing through a million hands."

Distrustful of everyone except his close circle of mostly women friends, and suddenly aware of his own mortality, he withdrew into a manufactured world.

Fascinated by Disneyland in Anaheim, he'd often disguise himself to spend time there among the robots and costumed actors. He even began constructing facsimiles of Disneyland rides, scenery and characters in the family's Encino home. The creations were overseen by his mother, Katherine, who divorced his father in 1982 and who had become a committed Jehovah's Witness.

"I'm putting all this stuff in," he said, "so I won't have to go out there."

Another installation was an extensive private zoo that sheltered a couple of fawns, a llama, a cougar, exotic birds and Jackson's pet boa constrictor, named Muscles. The boa's rippling, sinuous form inspired the titillating lyrics for the Diana Ross hit of the same name, written by Jackson in 1982.

Other animals would be added in time, fueling Jackson's passionate belief in their innate gentleness and understanding, qualities he believed children also possessed. Adults infuriated him. He said that their capacity for duplicity and phoniness made him "sick." Jackson opted for the shelter of his game room full of high-tech electronic toys and adorned with images of Peter Pan, his favorite fictional character. He often said he'd prefer a world inhabited only by children, and he often sought their company in times of stress.

During this period, Jackson also fell in love with *E.T., The Extraterrestrial*. In moviemaker Steven Spielberg's fantasy character, Jackson saw his own self-image: part alien, part human, part animal, part child, infinitely gentle and ingenuous yet profoundly wise and caring, lost but found. He saw the movie eight or ten times, he admitted. Then he opened negotiations with Spielberg and MCA Records to record a two-LP

Dark glasses all around; the glitter days.

Michael and Elizabeth Taylor at the American Music Awards in Los Angeles, 1985.

narrative of the story, incorporating John Williams' evocative score.

The project was completed, but it ended in failure when CBS was allowed an injunction against MCA for breach of contract. CBS argued that *The E.T. Storybook*, which was delayed in production, might detract from Jackson's upcoming solo album. Most of the 450,000 copies already released were withdrawn from sale.

As intriguing a personality as Jackson had become, nothing could have prepared the world for *Thriller*, launched in December 1982. Its impact was immediate and overpowering, beginning with a pre-release single, "The Girl Is Mine." A soppy, shallow collaboration with Paul McCartney, the song was inspired by the airy "society" movies of Fred Astaire.

Co-produced by Jackson and Quincy Jones, *Thriller* is a masterpiece of stylish songwriting, awesome interpretive abilities, conceptual integrity and compelling sonic artistry. Bulging with painful, post-adolescent angst, it quickly became a rites-of-passage testament for the millions who

Another part of him.

The gloved one works out.

Michael and Mickey Mouse greet admirers at the start of the BAD Tour in Tokyo.

identified with the mixed feelings of anticipation and horror that usher in adulthood.

Moreover, it shows Jackson's pre-eminence in the entertainment business, featuring contributions from premier rock guitarist Eddie Van Halen; Los Angeles session musicians and Toto band members Steve Lukather and Steve Porcaro; Quincy Jones; singer/songwriter James Ingram; Paul McCartney; veteran horror movie star Vincent Price; and master composer Rod Temperton. LaToya and Janet also appeared on the album.

But what has astonished critics most about *Thriller* is the assurance and self-revealing maturity of Jackson's three solo compositions — "Beat It," "Billie Jean" and "Wanna Be Startin' Something," a feisty, antagonistic threat against media gossips who "eat off you."

"Beat It" appeals for compassion and tolerance in the face of mounting acrimony between tribes, races, political juggernauts and opponents of all kinds who use violence to solve problems. Ironically, the message is underpinned by a vicious, spitting vocal and Van Halen's gritty, macho guitar riffs.

In "Billie Jean," Jackson cuts desperately close

Beating it.

to the bone, insisting with unusual passion that he is not the father of a child borne by a scheming, clinging woman. The song was echoed in a real-life incident in 1987, when 39-year-old Lavon Powlis Muhammad claimed in a $150 million paternity suit that her twin 6-year-olds resulted from a brief sexual liaison with Jackson. The case was thrown out of court.

Thriller was the best-selling album of 1983, hitting the top of the charts by the end of February and selling 16 million copies worldwide by the end of the year.

The videos of "Beat It" and "Billie Jean", both directed by Bob Giraldi, defined a new art form.

"Beat It," with its 200-member cast of dancing street-gangsters, resembled a modern day *West Side Story*. In "Billy Jean's" deliberate avoidance of a literal interpretation of the lyric, the video gave Jackson's character new depth. A challenging metaphor, it presented him almost as a figment of our imagination, as a sexually potent illusion whose presence is signified only in flashes of light, never in the flesh.

And the 14-minute mini-movie *Thriller* brought even greater possibilities to the medium. Costing $1 million, it was directed by *American Werewolf In London's* Jon Landis and choreographed by Broadway dance star Michael Peters. Eventually marketed as a home video, the mini-movie is credited with promoting sales of an additional eight million copies of the album in America alone.

Thriller became the focus of a kind of mass hysteria, which was stirred again in May, when Jackson took part in the TV special celebrating Motown's 25th anniversary. The show was viewed by 50 million Americans and tens of millions around the world. There, amid the cream of Motown's massive crop, reunited in pride and victory for a single event, Jackson was king. He was living proof and vindication of all the work and dreams of his fellow performers.

To cap off a spectacular year, Jackson received in 1984 eight Grammys, seven American Music Awards, four Black Gold Awards, four American Video Awards, three MTV Video Awards, The People's Choice Award for favorite all-round male entertainer and scores of similar awards from other countries.

Chapter 8

The Victory Tour

Though it would be The Jacksons' most successful album and it would lead to a tour that yielded the highest gross per capita in music history, *Victory* will be remembered largely as a catastrophe — and as the last formal collaboration between Michael Jackson and his brothers.

Preceded by a press conference in New York to announce their "reunion," at which an uncommunicative Michael Jackson seemed tense and distracted, *Victory* was seen as a promotional device for a final, take-the-money-and-run concert tour.

With precious little input from Michael Jackson ("State Of Shock," a duet with Mick Jagger, and "Be Not Always," a mediocre ballad, were his only contributions), the album received mixed reviews when released in June 1984. In addition, it was overshadowed by extraordinary turmoil involving the family business — just as the *Victory* tour was being planned.

Eccentric boxing entrepreneur Don King, inexperienced in concert events, was taken on

A victorious line-up.

Michael Jackson:
percussion personified.

Michael on his way to the Grammy's in 1984.

Michael with "serious" squeeze Brooke Shields.

The ultimate music man.

as tour promoter. But he never won Michael Jackson's confidence. Through a series of flips, the tour ended up in the hands of football promoter Chuck Sullivan, who guaranteed the family $38 million, or 85 percent of every ticket sold.

A few months earlier, Joe Jackson had handed the group's management over to former Epic promotions chief Frank Dileo, saying "the white input" of Weisner and DeMann during the first few years with CBS was no longer needed.

In a prepared statement, Michael Jackson lashed out at his father, and, though Dileo is also white and still represents the singer, things have never been quite as close between Joe and his son since.

"This (The Victory Tour) is our last and final tour."

Right from the cradle, the Jackson children were united by music.

"I happen to be color blind," Michael Jackson said. "I don't hire color. I hire competence...I have the final word on every decision. Racism is not my motto. One day I strongly expect every color to live as one family."

As the start of the tour approached, fans also began expressing their resentment at the "greed" of The Jacksons, (whose fee necessitated an abnormally high $30 ticket price), at the promoter's demand that tickets be sold in blocks of four and at the mail-order distribution method.

Again Michael Jackson came up front, demanding that the distribution and block-buying systems be abandoned. He could do nothing about the price of the tickets, but he let the fans know how he felt about it by announcing that he'd give all his tour earnings not to the family — but to charity.

If the *Victory* tour itself was less than it could have been, it still was a spectacle of unprecedented proportions featuring videos, special effects, giant illusions, fireworks and high-tech pomp and circumstance as a setting for the old-style Jacksons' revue and the spangled, one-gloved *Thriller* killer.

When *Victory* eventually stopped rolling, however, no one seemed more relieved than Michael Jackson. That was the past; he had other things on his mind.

Chapter 9   **The Superstar**

He's a performer who
lets the fans know how
he feels.

Michael Jackson:
reaching for it.

All the right moves.

"This is our last and final tour," he announced during the closing *Victory* concert at Dodger Stadium in Los Angeles in December 1984. "I mean, this is our farewell tour. You've all been wonderful. It's been a long 20 years and we love you all."

For the last couple of years, Michael Jackson, with the help of business manager John Branca, had worked steadily and quietly to expand his influence in the music business, in movies and in real estate. He had invested in a California-based company that developed new sound technology, in real estate properties all over the country, in the publication of catalogs (among them, the songs of Sly Stone), and in the production of videos. He had even signed a $300,000 deal with Doubleday book publishers to write his autobiography, with the help of celebrity editor, Jackie Onassis. And he was negotiating the biggest product endorsement deal in history with Pepsi Cola, which had already contributed $5 million to The Jacksons tour in exchange for performances in commercials. The company would be willing in 1988 to part with another $15 million for Michael Jackson alone.

Something was driving him past stardom, past his own sense of artistic perfection, to new regions. His friends said that he was striving for immortality. At one point in the past year, he'd

been reminded of his own physical vulnerability. He'd been frightened.

That was true. In January 1984, while shooting a Pepsi commercial with his brothers in the Los Angeles' Shrine Auditorium, his gelled hair was accidentally set on fire by exploding flashpots as he walked down a staircase miming an altered version of "Billie Jean."

"Tito! Tito!" he shouted to his brother, who was beside him. Tito and the others smothered the flames with their jackets. Their quick action averted a disaster; he was up and about within a week.

But who can imagine the terror in his heart and mind during those few seconds? Who can measure how deep the inner scars were and probably still are?

In many ways, Michael Jackson has not been the same person since that day.

In 1984 and '85, he was frequently seen among the upper echelon of Hollywood society — with Elizabeth Taylor and director Vincente Minnelli, Sophia Loren and Charlton Heston, with Brooke Shields and Jodie Foster, Sidney Poitier, Steven Spielberg and Francis Ford Coppola.

He was clearly a high-ranking member of America's show business royalty, though he was rarely seen or heard in public. He "came out" in January 1985, to galvanize some 40 of his musical peers in the "We Are The World" single and video. This massive project was inspired by British rocker Bob Geldof's Live Aid crusade to raise public consciousness and millions of dollars

Michael is a photographer's dream come true.

The "BAD" Boy belts it out.

for famine relief in Ethiopia.

Jackson and singer Lionel Richie co-wrote the "We Are The World" single, which was produced by Quincy Jones, under the group name USA For Africa. The session brought together such luminaries as Bob Dylan, Bruce Springsteen, Stevie Wonder, Bette Midler, Hall and Oates and Diana Ross.

It was a memorable effort and a cause for which Jackson no doubt cared deeply. Yet he appeared detached, as if he were above it all.

He may well have been distracted. By August that year, he had completed the intricate negotiations with Robert Holmes a Court that resulted in his taking over the 4,000-song ATV publishing catalog—complete with the crown jewels of the pop repertoire, the rights to The Beatles' 251-song collection.

He paid a price, of course—almost $50 million and the friendship of Paul McCartney, behind whose back he had worked and from whom he had learned the tricks of the trade. Ironically, just

10 months earlier, the two had released another syrupy collaboration, "Say, Say, Say."

To industry insiders, Jackson's move was a master stroke; only a handful of artists in any discipline have dared extend a passion for their work into the realm of business. He was instantly exalted to new heights, literally.

Under wraps, he had been working with film greats Francis Ford Coppola and George Lucas, the creator of *Star Wars*, and with the financial resources of the mammoth Disney studio. In September 1986, he disclosed his participation in bringing a new kind of thriller to Florida's Disney World and California's Disneyland. It was *Captain Eo* — a 16-minute, 3-D, multi-screen science fiction fantasy directed by Lucas, produced by Coppola and starring Anjelica Huston as an evil empress and Jackson as an omnipotent warrior whose mission is to redeem order and peace to the universe. It cost $17 million to make, and it suited Jackson's sense of morality. Conceptually, *Captain Eo* was "Beat It" in another dimension.

In the meantime, Jackson was under wraps of another kind. Though manager Frank Dileo publicly denied it and threatened to sue anyone who said Jackson was undergoing prosthetic

...And maturity.

Michael's endorsement is announced.

On his own but never alone.

surgery, it was obvious (and not just because of the surgical mask he occasionally wore) that his features had been and were still changing.

He wanted to make himself over, it seemed, in the image of a raceless, sexless, eternally youthful being. His eccentricity and acquisitive urge knew no bounds during 1986 and '87. He bought another 90-acre property nearby and he was often seen traveling between the house and the front gate on a full-sized locomotive. He purchased a hyperbaric chamber (into which pure oxygen is pumped to help treat burn victims and disease cases), believing it would help him live to 150. He apparently horrified his business partners by saying that he wanted to take the chamber with him on tour.

He also offered a British museum $1.3 million — an unsuccessful attempt to obtain the preserved remains of John Merrick, the grotesquely disfigured "Elephant Man" of Victorian England, who died in 1900. No reasons were given for Jackson's interest in Merrick; but given his sentimental heart and the humiliation Merrick suffered as a circus and scientific freak, there's no doubt that the wealthy young star felt he'd found another kindred soul.

Thriller's fire and Grimstone.

An almost religious intensity.

Instead, he picked up a male chimpanzee, Bubbles, who would keep his company on tour.

Besides all this, Jackson continued working toward a serious post-*Thriller* career in music. It seemed impossible for him to top that landmark achievement—the best-selling record in history.

Work on 1987's *Bad* album prompted a breach with the Jehovah's Witnesses and symbolized a profound shift in Jackson's values. He could no longer reconcile the church's demands that followers lead a quiet life with the pace and demands of his own. Without comment, he allowed himself to be dissociated.

Many observers, notably those who had ridiculed him the most for his religious beliefs, took this news as further proof that possessions and wealth, not the welfare of man, now consumed him. Soon, as additional evidence of Jackson's self-aggrandizing need for excess, they were pointing to his association with movie director Martin Scorsese on a 14-minute, $3-million video for the album's title track.

And in August 1987, when the *Bad* album and video were unveiled, reaction was almost universally poor. Some critics pointed out that the video was racist because it implied that black kids were street hoodlums. Jackson, whose manufactured features in the black-and-white "story" section of the video looked hideously alien, was hardly an example of the philosophy *Bad* was supposed to impart: That success is a matter of self-help and education, regardless of color or circumstances.

Moreover, the term "bad" is an expression that's no longer part of the current black street vernacular. And the leather-and-buckles style that Jackson had suddenly adopted was seen as outdated at best, sexually problematic at worst; he had simply proven how out of touch he was with the real world.

In spite of the critics' initial reaction, *Bad* won favor with a suspicious public within just a few weeks. Co-produced again by Jackson and Quincy Jones, the album features vocal contributions from Stevie Wonder and gospel star Andrae Crouch. Eight of its ten cuts were written by Jackson, the greatest number he has contributed to any album — proof of his confidence and maturity.

The video aside, self-improvement is a convincing and recurring theme, from the gentle "Man In The Mirror" (a non-original) to "Dirty Diana" (a cynical apologia that barely conceals a groupie's self-disgust at being someone's "night lovin' thing...the freak you can taunt") and "Another Part Of Me" (which emphasizes our common humanity).

And despite the fact that *Bad* was shut out at the 1988 Grammys, Jackson nonetheless drew a lengthy standing ovation for a rousing, gospel-tinged version of "Man In The Mirror."

Above all, the humanity that *Bad* represents is the gem that remains at the core of his concert performances — and of all his work.

Somehow, when he shows what's in his heart, Michael Jackson doesn't seem so much a fantasy after all.

GREG QUILL is an entertainment writer and music critic for the *Toronto Star*. During the 1970s he was a songwriter/guitarist fronting bands in Canada and his native Australia, where he recorded several albums and had a number of chart successes. Many of his songs have been recorded by other Australian artists, as well as American and British performers.

Quill holds a BA in English Language and Literature from the University of Sydney, and was the first rock songwriter in his country to be awarded a travel/study grant by the Australian Council for the Arts.

He has written feature articles, reviews and opinion pieces for several Canadian magazines since settling in Toronto in 1976, and he edited the Canadian rock publications *Music Express* (now *Rock Express*) and *Graffiti* in the early 1980s.

Quill quit performing and recording in 1982, and is at present working on a book of short stories and a screenplay set in the music business. His most recent book for Goddard & Kamin Inc. was on Bon Jovi in 1987.

PHOTOGRAPHERS

Color:
Kate Simon/STAR FILE; **C.B. Blum, Hollis, C. Ruby, Paul Slattery**/RETNA LTD.;
Eugene Adebari, Torin Boyd, Collette (SHOOTING STAR), **Sam Emerson**/PONO PRESSE.

Black & White:
Richard E. Aaron, Bob Gruen, J. Jay, Chuck Pulin, Bob Scott, Vinnie Zuffante/STAR FILE;
C.B. Blum/RETNA LTD.

Goddard & Kamin Inc. is one of the world's leading packagers and publishers of mass market books. Peter Goddard and Philip Kamin first got together in 1981 for a book on the Rolling Stones' last tour. Since then they have combined to produce more than 50 titles.